BOOK OF
TOMATOES

NATIONAL **Gardening** ASSOCIATION

BOOK OF

TOMATOES

Edited by the staff of the
National Gardening magazine

ILLUSTRATIONS BY
ELAYNE SEARS & LYN SEVERANCE

VILLARD BOOKS ▪ NEW YORK ▪ 1987

Library of Congress Catalogue
Card Number: 86-40340

ISBN 0-394-75000-4

Designed by Joel Avirom

Manufactured in the United States of America
9 8 7 6 5 4 3 2
Revised Edition

CONTENTS

BOOK OF
TOMATOES

TOMATO VARIETIES

If you're just starting a small backyard or community garden, try growing just a few tomato plants at first—perhaps four to eight plants of two to three different varieties. If you choose varieties that mature at different times, you can stretch your harvest over many weeks. If you are buying seeds to start your own plants, read catalog descriptions carefully to find out when different varieties ripen. Nursery-grown plants are often labeled *early*, *midseason*, or *late* to indicate their ripening period.

Another consideration in choosing tomato varieties is whether they are *determinate* or *indeterminate* type vines. Determinate plants grow to a certain height and then stop. Because of their more restrained size, determinate varieties often need no staking. They set all their fruit within a relatively short period of time—usually about a week to ten days. This can be a boon if you are canning, but for the gardener who prefers to have a fewer number of tomatoes over a longer period of time, indeterminate varieties are better. These continue to grow in height throughout the season and set fruits over a longer period of time.

The following chart lists some of the more popular tomato varieties available today. There are many more, of course, and plenty of them would probably do well in your garden. Talk to your local county extension agent and to other home gardeners to find out which varieties are tried-and-true performers in your part of the country.

When selecting a tomato variety, keep in mind what you plan to do with the tomatoes. There are varieties suited for just about every purpose—eating fresh, making tomato paste, canning, and for growing in pots and other small containers.

Seeds, Seeds, Seeds

EARLY SEASON (50–65 days from transplanting)

Variety	Resist-ance	Growth Pattern	Comments
Burpee's Big Early		Ind	Early-ripening rugged hybrid
Early Girl (HY)	V	Ind	4–6 oz tomatoes; stake or cage
Fireball		Det	4-oz fruits; sets in cool weather
New Yorker	V	Det	Widely recommended; 6-oz fruits
Pixie (HY)		Det	Very early; sets fruit in cool weather
Spring Giant	VF	Det	High yields; large fruits
Springset	VF	Det	Widely adapted; short harvest
Starfire		Det	6-oz. fruits

MIDSEASON (65–75 days)

Variety	Resist-ance	Growth Pattern	Comments
Avalanche (HY)	F	Ind	Very crack-resistant
Better Boy (HY)	VFN	Ind	Widely recommended and adapted, but susceptible to blossom end rot
Bonny Best		Ind	Old-time favorite in South
Burpee's Big Boy (HY)		Ind	Very popular, large 12-oz fruits. Long producer

Burpee's Big Girl (HY)	VF	Ind	Like Big Boy, but has resistance
Burpee's VF (HY)	VF	Ind	Widely recommended; resistant to cracking and catfacing
Campbell 1327	VF	Det	Set fruits in adverse conditions
Celebrity (HY)	VFN	Det	Large (8–12 oz) fruits
Floradel	VF	Ind	Stage or cage. Crack-resistant
Floramerica (HY)	VF	Det	Compact growth. Tolerant to many diseases
Heinz 1350	VF	Det	Productive canning tomato
Jet Star (HY)	VF	Ind	Widely recommended; 8-oz fruits
Longkeeper			Best harvested at partially ripe stage for storage up to 12 weeks
Manapal	F	Ind	Bred for humid conditions. Good Southern variety
Marglobe	F	Det	Old favorite. Smooth, firm, 6-oz fruits
Moreton Hybrid	VF	Ind	6–8 oz fruits; Northeast favorite
Rutgers	F	Ind	Large 6–8 oz fruits
Super Sioux		Semi-det	Widely adapted sets; fruit in high temp
Supersonic (HY)	VF	Semi-det	Widely recommended

LATESEASON (80–90 days)

Variety	Resist-ance	Growth Pattern	Comments
Manalucie	F	Ind	Grows well in adverse conditions; widely recommended in South
Oxheart		Ind	Heart-shaped tomatoes up to 2 lbs
Ramapo (HY)	VF	Ind	Sets well in adverse conditions. Resistant to cracking, blossom end rot
Wonder Boy (HY)	VF	Ind	Heavy producer of 8-oz tomatoes

BEEFSTEAK VARIETIES (large tomatoes; 80–90 days)

Variety	Resist-ance	Growth Pattern	Comments
Beefmaster (HY)	VFN	Det	Hefty fruits; up to 2 lbs
Pink Ponderosa		Ind	Meaty, firm tomatoes. Cage plants to protect from sunscald

YELLOW ORANGE VARIETIES (80–85 days)

Variety	Resist-ance	Growth Pattern	Comments
Golden Boy (HY)	VFN	Det	Somewhat lower acid tomato
Jubilee		Ind	
Sunray	F	Ind	

PASTE VARIETIES (75–80 days)

Variety	Resist-ance	Growth Pattern	Comments
Roma	VF	Det	Widely recommended
San Marzano		Ind	Quite popular canner

CHERRY AND CONTAINER VARIETIES (45–60 days)

Variety	Resist-ance	Growth Pattern	Comments
Burgess Early Salad (HY)		Det	Plant grows only 8 inches tall, but good producer
Patio Hybrid	F	Det	2-inch tomatoes; 70 days to maturity
Pixie Hybrid		Det	Great early variety for garden or sunny window. Fruits larger than cherry types.
Small Fry (HY)	VFN	Det	Heavy producer of small fruits. Plant in garden or 5-gallon container
Sweet 100 (HY)		Ind	Stake or cage; many 1 oz fruits
Tiny Tim		Det	¾ inch fruits. Great for pots, windowsills.

KEY TO CHART

V = Resistance to verticillium wilt.

F = Resistance to fusarium wilt.

N = Resistance to nematodes and root-knot problems.

Det = Bush or determinate type of growth. Terminal leader or main stem develops a flower bud at top of its growth.

Ind = Tall growing or indeterminate type of growth, good for staking, caging, or trellising. Terminal leader does not develop a flower bud, allowing continued vegetable growth.

HY = Hybrid variety.

ON YOUR WAY

Most gardeners transplant young nursery-grown or home-started tomato seedlings when all danger of frost has passed and the soil has warmed up, rather than sowing seeds directly in the garden. In southern Florida, parts of California, and the Southwest, gardeners can set out tomato plants in the fall for a winter harvest.

If you buy your plants, you may not have a wide choice of varieties. Starting your own plants from seed lets you choose from an almost endless list of varieties. You must be able to provide proper growing conditions to produce strong healthy transplants, however. Seeds should be

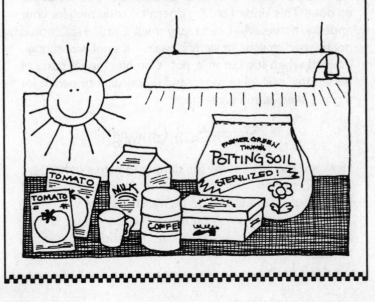

started six to eight weeks before the last frost date in your area. Here's what you'll need:

Tomato seeds.

Seed starting trays or "flats" or other containers, such as paper cups, milk cartons, or peat pots. Just be sure there are holes in the bottom for drainage.

Adequate light for the seedlings—either sunlight or fluorescent. Regular fluorescent lights work fine.

Pasteurized soil mix.

A NOTE ON SOIL

The soil mixes available in most garden stores are very good. They are pasteurized, that is, free of weed seeds and disease-causing fungi that can cause young seedlings to collapse and die—a problem called "damping off."

If you're thinking about using garden soil to start your plants, you should pasteurize it first. You can do this by baking it in the oven at 200° in a shallow pan for about an hour. This kind of baking doesn't do anything for your appetite, however—it can really smell. Garden soil should not be used straight for starting seeds—it's not well enough drained when it's put in a pot. Combine equal parts of pasteurized soil, peat moss, and vermiculite or perlite for a good seed-starting soil mix.

Step-by-Step Growing

Here are the basic steps for starting tomato seeds:

1. Moisten the soil mix, put it in your container, and level it out. The soil should be moist, but not wet.

2. Sprinkle the seeds on top of the soil, about ½ inch apart. They can be scattered over the surface or placed in rows.

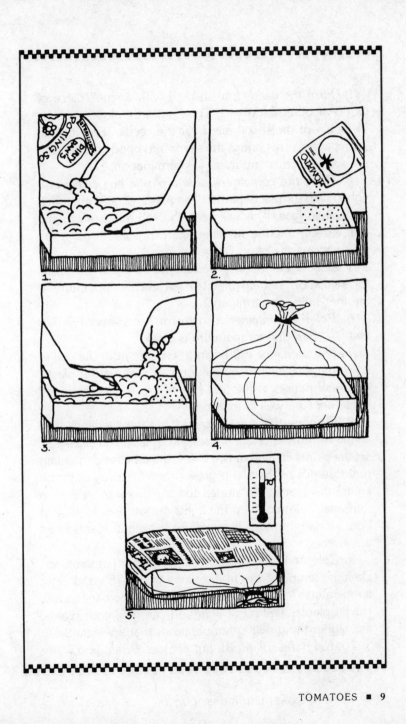

3. *Firm the seeds* into the soil with a small piece of wood or other flat object. Then put a thin layer—about ¼ inch—of moist soil mix over the seeds, level it, then firm it again. This brings the seeds into good contact with the soil, which is important for germination.

4. *Place the container inside a plastic bag* or cover it tightly with a sheet of plastic. The plastic should not touch the soil surface. This will keep the soil mix from drying out. As soon as the seedlings start to poke through the soil, remove the plastic cover.

5. *Place a few sheets of newspaper on top* of the plastic for insulation to help maintain an even temperature—another help for germination.

6. *Put the container in a warm spot*—about 70° is ideal—where the temperature is even.

7. *The seedlings will begin to emerge from the soil in a few days.* Check daily so you can remove the plastic and newspapers at the first sign of green and move the container to a well-lit location.

8. *Remove the coverings* and put the seedlings in a sunny window or under fluorescent lights. If you use lights, set the plants an inch or two below the tubes and maintain that distance as the plants grow. If too far away from the lights, the plants will stretch toward them and develop thin, weak stems. Keep the lights on fourteen to sixteen hours a day, but turn them off for the night. Plants need a rest, too!

9. *Give your seedlings proper growing temperatures.* Daytime temperatures in the range of 60–75°, and night temperatures in the range of 60–65°, will encourage sturdy, stocky plants. The more light you can give your plants, the higher the growing temperatures that are suitable.

10. *Keep the soil moist, but not wet.* When you water

the plants, do it gently so you don't wash any of them out. Try to use room temperature water, if possible.

11. Don't worry about fertilizing the seedlings right away. Some commercial seed-starting mixes have fertilizer mixed in that will take care of the seedlings' nutritional needs while they are small. Otherwise, wait at least a week—or even until after the first repotting—before feeding plants. Then apply a balanced, water-soluble fertilizer diluted to one-quarter strength in with the plants' water once a week.

The First Repotting—A Must!

When the seedlings are 3 or 4 inches tall and have their second pair of leaves, it's time to take them out of their crowded containers and put them into deeper, roomier containers. (If you started seedlings in individual containers at least 3 inches square, simply thin out the weaker plants, leaving the one strongest.)

Since any part of the tomato stem covered with soil will develop more roots (and a large root system is important for transplants), one of the basic rules about trans-

planting tomatoes is to use a deeper container and set the plants lower than they were growing before. Pick off all but the top four leaves and set the plants in the soil right up to those upper leaves. Use the same pasteurized soil mix that you started your seeds in for repotting. Here are some hints for successful repotting:

Water the tomatoes well the evening before you start to repot. Moist soil will stick to the roots and protect them from drying out.

Lever the seedlings out of the soil with a small utensil —a table knife is handy for this. Hold the plants by their leaves, if necessary, rather than by their stems to prevent crushing delicate tissues.

Set the seedlings about 3 inches apart in their new container(s). Firm the soil around them, and water gently. Keep out of bright sunlight for a day or two.

Fertilize once a week. Use a complete water-soluble fertilizer diluted to about one-third the strength recommended on the package.

Moving Time Again

Before the tomatoes can be transplanted successfully in the garden, the seedlings need to develop strong root and top growth. To be sure they have a good root system, many gardeners prefer to transplant their tomatoes a second time before setting them out in the garden. Wait until seedings are 6 to 10 inches tall. Then transplant individually into half-gallon milk cartons. Pick off all but the top two to four leaves, and set the plants as deeply as possible. New roots will develop all along the part of the stem that is now buried in the soil.

Indoor Care

Many gardeners often have a problem with leggy seedlings. This condition is caused by too much fertilizer, too warm temperatures, or too little light (or a combination of these factors). If your seedlings are leggy, go back over the growing steps to see how you can improve conditions for your plants. Transplanting leggy seedlings deeply will help to reduce the problem, but the best solution is to give your young plants proper growing conditions in the first place.

A Note on Shopping for Transplants

When you buy tomato transplants at a garden store, supermarket, or roadside stand, take the time to pick out the best plants. Look for plants with thick stems—the thicker the better—and with large root systems, best indicated by a dark-green plant in a deep container. The tallest transplants are not necessarily the best ones. And don't pick out a plant with blossoms or fruits. Unless it's in a deep pot, it won't have a strong enough root system to support the fruit yet.

Be wary of plants with blemishes or poor color. Also, check the undersides of the leaves for aphids (small, pear-shaped insects) or tiny whiteflies. These are pests you don't want to bring near your garden. They multiply rapidly and can cause lots of problems.

"Hardening Off" Transplants

Tomato plants—no matter if they're bought in a store or home-grown—must be toughened up or "hardened off" before you plant them in the garden. After all, they've been indoors for six to eight weeks and they're quite tender. They will get sunburned or windburned if they're transplanted before they are accustomed to the outdoors. The extra time and care you devote to readying your plants for their new outdoor home will really pay off.

It takes about ten days or so to harden tomato plants. The process of hardening a plant involves reducing the temperature of its environment by moving it outside, holding back water, and gradually exposing it to bright outdoor sunshine. The plant won't grow too much during this period; instead it is storing food to use when it needs it—during transplanting.

A few days before you are ready to begin hardening

plants off, cut back on the amount of water you give them, and stop fertilizing completely. On the first day of the hardening process, take the plants outside for a few hours and place them where they'll be protected from direct sun and wind. Each day lengthen the time outside a little, gradually exposing them to more sunshine and breeze. After a few days, leave them out all day and, a few days after that, all night as well. But if there is a chance of a frost, don't risk it—bring them indoors.

If you harden plants well, you won't have to take the trouble at planting time to protect the seedlings from sun and wind with all sorts of contraptions such as hot caps, milk jugs, etc. You've done the job already.

GARDEN PREPARATION

Where you plant your tomatoes in the garden is important. Tomatoes need at least six to eight hours of sun a day to produce well—and full sun is best, especially in cooler, more northern climates. Tomato roots will not do well in soggy soil—a sunny, well-drained part of your garden is best.

Tomatoes like their soil pH around 6.0–6.8. Briefly, pH is a measure of soil acidity or alkalinity. On the pH scale, 7.0 is neutral; so the range which tomatoes prefer is slightly on the acid side. (By the way, that's the pH range at which most vegetables grow best.)

You should check the pH level in your garden at least every three to five years. You can test it with an inexpensive kit from a garden store, or your local cooperative extension service may offer a low-priced testing service.

If your soil pH is too low (too acid), you'll need to add lime to the soil to bring the pH back into proper range. Gardeners in western states (and some areas of the east) often have high pH or alkaline soils; some of them need to add sulfur to the soil to lower the pH. Although lime and sulfur can be added to the soil any time of the year that the ground is not frozen, fall is a convenient time for many gardeners and gives slow-acting lime a chance to take effect. Get recommendations from the extension service on how much lime or sulfur to apply based on your soil test report.

Better Soil

No matter what kind of soil you have in your garden, you can shape it into a great home for your tomatoes with a little work. Both light, sandy soils that drain too rapidly and heavy, clay soils that take forever to drain and warm up in the spring can be improved with the addition of plenty of organic matter—leaves, compost, grass clippings, garden residues, or easy-to-grow cover crops such as buckwheat, cowpeas, or annual ryegrass.

In sandy soils, organic matter builds up the water-holding capacity of the soil, which is vitally important for tomatoes that depend on a continuous supply of moisture all season long. But tomatoes don't want to sit in puddles! Organic matter opens up heavy soil so that water and air penetrate better.

If your tomato crop has been only so-so for the past few years, work some extra organic matter into the soil where your plants will be growing. You'll probably see a big difference in the harvest.

It's also important to work the soil before transplanting time until it's loose to a depth of at least 6 to 8 inches. You can do the work with a garden tiller or a digging fork. The tomato roots will be able to expand quickly in the loose earth and you'll also uproot and kill many weeds by working the soil.

Fertilizer

It's important to work some fertilizer into the soil at transplanting time, so that your transplants can get off to a good start.

After the soil has been well tilled and is loose, make

a trench or furrow about 6 to 8 inches deep down what will be the row of tomatoes. At the bottom of the furrow first put a thin band of commercial fertilizer, such as 5-10-10. (Incidentally, the numbers 5-10-10 refer to the percentages, by weight, of nitrogen [N], phosphorus [P] and potassium [K] in the bag of fertilizer. They'll always be listed in that order, too: N-P-K.)

Another method is to put down a deeper band of organic fertilizer, such as dehydrated animal manure, as well as additional organic matter including compost or rotted leaves—whatever is on hand.

Then—no matter which method you have chosen—cover all this fertilizer with 2 or 3 inches of soil. You don't want the roots or stems of any transplants to come in direct contact with the fertilizer. If the roots come in direct contact with fresh fertilizer, the salts in the fertilizer can draw moisture from them, which is harmful. If the fertilizer is deep underneath the plant, then the roots will grow to it and absorb the nutrients gradually.

After covering the fertilizer, it's just a matter of transplanting the tomatoes into the furrow, which is now 3 or 4 inches deep.

TRANSPLANTING

You're the Boss

As a gardener, you must realize that each season some things are simply out of your control—rainfall and sunshine, for example. But at a very important time in the life of your tomatoes—transplanting time—you're the boss.

Make no mistake about it—transplanting is a major step. If you do it carefully and use a little extra time and care, you can look forward to a crop that will be on time—or even ahead of everybody else's—healthy, and prolific.

Mistakes, such as rushing your plants into the ground before they are properly hardened, or roughing up the tomato roots when you're handling them, can really set the crop back.

So let's look at some of the general guidelines for transplanting methods, step by step, so you can decide which is the best way for you to transplant tomatoes.

Transplant tomatoes (and other crops, too) on a cloudy day or in the late afternoon or evening if you can. Bright sun can harm newly planted transplants.

Soak the transplants with water in their flats an hour before transplanting. This will help keep the soil around the roots and protect them, and the root mass will be easier to handle.

Have everything ready before taking the plants out of the flats. Have the soil prepared, the fertilizer applied in the furrow or in the holes, all tools at hand, etc.

Don't put too much fertilizer under the plants. One of the big mistakes people make is to toss too much fertilizer in the hole before they put their tomatoes in. Excessive fertilizer shocks and burns plants. It's better to hold off and give them extra nourishment later when they are established.

Protect against cutworms. Before putting the tomato plant in the ground, wrap a newspaper collar around the stem to protect the plant against cutworms. These ground-level pests can chew completely through the thin tomato stem. The collar should span from an inch or two above the soil surface to an inch below the cutworm's territory.

The newspaper collars are easy to put on and last long enough for the stems to thicken enough to discourage the cutworms. Tight collars of plastic can restrict the stem growth, so never use them.

Cup the roots in one hand when you take a transplant out of its container. To protect roots from needless exposure, work quickly. A smooth and speedy transition from flat to soil means less of a shock to the plant.

Keep transplants watered. They need water in the beginning to help them get over the shock of being transplanted, to encourage new root growth, and to replace the moisture they give off or "transpire" because of heat or drying winds.

Trouble-Free Transplanting

If you talk to many gardeners, you'll quickly get the notion there are as many methods, tips, and tricks to the art of transplanting as there are ways of baking a cake.

But despite all the variations—which give tomato growers so much to talk about—there are just a couple of basic ways to transplant.

Trench-Planting

In trench-planting, you simply pinch off all the lower leaves of the tomato plant and lay the whole plant in a shallow trench *horizontally*. Then cover the stem with 2 or 3 inches of soil and bring just the top cluster of leaves above the surface.

There are several advantages to this system. For one thing, additional roots will form all along the buried stem. The plant can take up more water and nutrients and get off to a quicker start.

Also, setting the roots only a few inches from the surface helps them to warm up quickly—and the heat-loving tomato plants appreciate that. When the rays of the sun hit the soil early in the morning, the roots start to feel the heat. That wouldn't happen if they were set deep in a hole. The extra heat the shallow roots receive gets them off to a strong start and speeds up the first harvest.

Though you might think only northern gardeners with short seasons would be interested in trench-planting, its practical in the South, too. Because it gets too hot in the middle of the summer in some parts of the South for tomatoes to do well, gardeners try to plant early so they can harvest before summer heat slows up production. Trench-planting helps their tomatoes get a quicker start than if they were planted vertically in deep, cool spring soil.

How to Trench-Plant

When the trench is dug, fertilizer added and covered, and everything else is ready, carefully take the tomato plant out of its container, cupping your hand around the root-ball. Try to disturb the soil covering the roots as little as possible. Pinch off the lower leaves of the plant, leaving just the top cluster of leaves.

Then wrap a newspaper cutworm collar (see page 20 for more on this) around the top of the stem and lay the plant down in the trench horizontally. Quickly cover the roots and entire length of stem up to the leaves with 2 or 3 inches of soil and firm it down.

Don't try to bend the top of the plant up—just push a little pillow of soil underneath to support it. Mother Nature will see that it grows up in the right direction.

Give the area a good soaking after the seedlings are in place.

Space the plants so that the top clusters of leaves showing above the surface are 36 to 48 inches apart. You can put them closer if you plan on staking them—18 to 24 inches. Leave about 3 feet of space between the rows so you can cultivate and later get around the plants to prune and harvest.

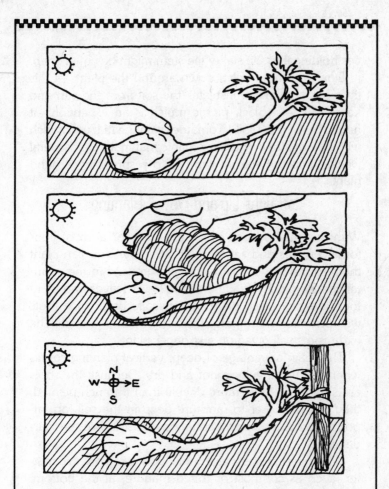

Planting time is the time to stake your trench-planted tomatoes because you know where the long stem is underground. If your garden is in a windy spot, put the stakes on the side of the plants opposite the prevailing winds. If winds come from the west, for example, place the stake on the east side of the plants. Then, when the wind blows the plant will be held against the stake. Otherwise, if the wind pushes the plant against the string or ties holding it to the stake, the stem might be cut or snap.

Don't put any mulch down around the plants at this time because mulch insulates the soil from the sun and keeps it cool. (Black plastic mulch is an exception—it helps to warm the soil.) Tomatoes want heat! If you mulch with hay or straw or other organic materials, wait several weeks until the soil is warm before spreading around plants.

Straight Up-and-Down Planting

With this method you prepare a hole for each of your tomato plants and set them in vertically. You can plant them to the same level they were growing in their containers, or pinch off some of the lower leaves and plant them deeply. Deep planting is usually best, since roots will form along any part of the stem that is buried. The extra roots will give you a stronger plant.

The main advantage of deep, vertical planting comes when the weather gets hot and dry. Because the roots are set in and grow more deeply than if trench-planted, they will be closer to moisture deep in the soil, an important consideration for southern and southwestern gardeners.

When you prepare each hole, add some organic matter, such as compost or rotted manure, at the bottom. This will increase the moisture-holding ability of the soil and also allow the roots to expand easily. When you put fertilizer in the hole, be sure to mix it with some soil and cover it with 2 or 3 inches of additional soil before setting in the plant.

Space plants 18 to 24 inches apart if you plan on staking them. If you plan to let them sprawl, give them more room—36 to 48 inches. Space rows 3 feet apart.

STAKING, CAGING, AND TRELLISING

It's often said that tomatoes will grow like weeds—they'll keep sending out new stems and branching out all over the place. Every time you turn around the plants are bigger and bushier.

To keep them from gobbling up too much garden space and to insure cleaner, healthier tomatoes, many gardeners support their plants, train them to grow a certain way, and regularly pinch off unwanted growth. Stakes, trellises, and cages are the most popular supports these days.

To Stake or Not to Stake

ADVANTAGES OF STAKING

Saves space. You can grow more plants in a given area.

Keeps vines and tomatoes off the ground. Fruit is cleaner with less rotting.

Earlier harvest. The pruning that staked tomatoes require forces more of the plant's energy into ripening fruit.

Each tomato is larger than if not staked. Pruned plants put more energy into fewer tomatoes.

Easier to pick tomatoes and to work around plants.

DISADVANTAGES OF STAKING

Takes time and effort to stake, train, and prune plants.

Tomatoes are more susceptible to cracking, blossom

end rot, and sunscald problems.

The total yield of staked plants is often lower than similar plants that are not staked. You have to prune off side shoots and branches to support the plant with a stake, and that actually reduces the total leaf surface of the plant. Since the leaf surface is the site of the plant's food-manufacturing operation, less leaf surface means a smaller total food supply, and that affects total yield.

Staked plants usually need mulching with materials such as hay or grass clippings. The mulch helps retain moisture in the soil. Staked plants actually need more water than unstaked tomatoes because they are held up and exposed to the sun and drying winds.

Not all tomato plants need staking. A tomato with what we call a determinate growth habit stops growing at a certain height—usually when it's fairly short. It stops growing because the main stem forms a flower bud at the top that produces fruit. Most of the determinate varieties are early types, and they are bushy plants with short, stout stems that support them pretty well. Some popular determinate varieties include *Spring Set, New Yorker, Spring Giant,* and *Fireball.*

Tomatoes with an indeterminate growth habit will continue to grow in height throughout the season if you feed them well and let them take off. You may see a photograph in the newspaper during the summer of a tomato plant being trained up the side of a house. The plant may be anywhere from 6 to 15 or 20 feet high. That's a well-fed indeterminate plant, for sure!

Many seed catalogs mention whether plants are determinate or indeterminate. This not only helps you decide whether or not you need to support your plants, but gives you an idea of the length of the harvest season.

Determinate varieties tend to set all their fruits within a relatively short period of time, while indeterminate varieties set a smaller number of fruits at one time, but do so over a longer period of time. If you're buying transplants and you're not sure what the growth habit is of the variety you've selected, by all means ask the salesperson or grower!

How to Stake

As we mentioned earlier, when you support a tomato, try to put the support on the prevailing downwind side of the plant so that the plant will be against the support when the wind is blowing hard.

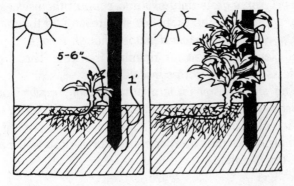

Stakes 6 to 8 feet high are good for most tomatoes, although you can make do with shorter 4- to 5-foot stakes, if necessary. Put the stakes in right after you've put the plants in the ground. Drive them about 1 foot deep in the soil, about 3 to 5 inches away from the plant. Of course, you don't put the stake on the root side of the tomatoes you've trench-planted. As the plant grows, tie a strip of cloth or nylon stocking or *coated* wire tightly to the stake and loosely around the plant in a figure-eight fashion. Leave at least an inch or two of slack. Add more ties as needed as the plant grows up the stake.

Supporting Tomatoes with Cages

One of the simplest ways to support plants is with cages—tall cylinders of wire mesh. Cages have more advantages than just being easy to use.

ADVANTAGES OF CAGING

Less time removing suckers, pruning branches, or training the plants up the cage. Most of the time you leave the plant alone.

The plants grow naturally and support themselves as they get big and the branches start resting on the mesh.

Caged tomato plants develop enough foliage to provide plenty of shade for ripening the fruit. The shade protects tomatoes from sunscald.

The shaded soil underneath the plant retains more moisture. Even moisture in the soil reduces blossom end rot and cracking problems. That's especially important for central and southern gardeners with brilliant sunshine and hot, dry weather.

DISADVANTAGES OF CAGING

Cages cost money.

How to Cage

Garden stores sell tomato cages, but you can easily make your own. They should be strong, at least 5 feet tall (to handle most varieties), with holes big enough to get your

hand in to bring out nice, big tomatoes! Otherwise, it looks a little odd heading out to pick tomatoes with a pair of wire cutters!

Sturdy galvanized wire mesh is a good choice for making cages that you can use for years. The cages can be from 12 to 30 inches in diameter; use the larger cages for vigorous, indeterminate-type plants. You need about 3 feet of mesh for every 1-foot diameter of cage. Fasten the cages on two sides to short stakes driven into the ground to prevent them from toppling over.

Fencing only a foot or two high can be used to hold up shorter determinate varieties such as *New Yorker* and *Pixie*. (Use smaller diameter cages for these varieties.) Though it is not necessary to support these varieties, you'll probably get more rot-free tomatoes by using short cages.

Extra Mileage from Cages

Here's an easy way to give your caged tomato transplants a boost early in the season. (With a couple of twists, you can adapt the following suggestions to plants you're growing with other supports, or even if you're leaving them unstaked.)

When you put the tomato plants in the ground, set the cages over them immediately and secure the cages with small stakes or push them firmly into the ground if you can.

Then make a tight circle of 1-foot-high black felt roofing paper (or dark plastic) around the outside of the cage at ground level. Staple the overlapping ends of the paper together.

The black paper will gather heat for the tomato plants—they appreciate it early in the season—and it will also protect the plants from bruising winds.

If you don't use cages, rig up some kind of support system for the black paper—maybe using cut coat hangers—so that the paper stands straight around the plants. Keep it about 8 to 10 inches away from the plants.

Researchers recently studied this method of aiding caged plants in Texas and saw yield increases of 25 to 50 percent over unprotected plants of the same variety.

It's pretty easy to find inexpensive roofing paper. Most lumber and building stores have it. You can probably get some free from scrap piles at construction sites.

Trellising

Trellising can be creative and attractive, but it can also be a lot of work.

ADVANTAGES OF TRELLISING

Trellises require little space, and tomatoes can be planted closer together.

Fruit ripens earlier.

DISADVANTAGES OF TRELLISING

Necessary to build support system, using slats of wood, wire-mesh fencing, pipes, or poles and wire.

More time necessary for pruning and training—at least some time required each week.

Fewer tomatoes because of pruning.

Greater sunscald susceptibility because of less shade from leafy growth.

How to Trellis

A good trellising system is one using 4-foot stakes placed 5 feet apart down the row with three wires running horizontally between them, a foot above one another.

As the tomatoes start to grow, train them so their branches interweave around and through the wires. Train two or three main stems per plant, and keep all the other side shoots picked off. These shoots that spring up right above the crotch where the branches grow from the main stem are called "suckers." Tie some of the stems to the wires for extra support.

When the tallest branch grows beyond the top wire,

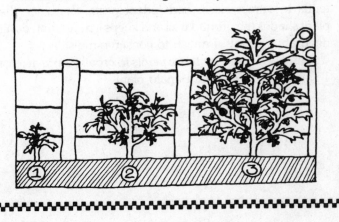

cut it off. This stops the branch from getting any higher. If it grows too far over the upper wire, it will break off anyway.

A Word on Free-Growing Tomatoes

Now that you've heard all about staking, caging, and trellising, here are some things to think about if you plan to let your tomato plants sprawl:

ADVANTAGES OF FREE-GROWING

No doubt about it, this method saves work. No stakes or supports to set up, no training the plants, and much less pruning to do.

A bigger tomato crop is possible because the plants bush out quite a bit, develop plenty of leaf surface, and extra tomatoes will form on the well-developed side stems.

DISADVANTAGES OF FREE-GROWING

You'll probably need a light mulch to keep the tomatoes from resting on the ground, where they're prone to rot or nibbles from insects and animals. Mulch, though, tends to attract insect and rodent pests. But since the plant shades the ground well and keeps it moist, you don't need a whole lot of mulch to conserve moisture.

You need room for these plants to grow. Figure at least 1 square yard for each tomato plant.

PRUNING

Never Give a Sucker an Even Break!

Pruning means pinching off the shoots or "suckers" that grow out from the stem in the crotch right above a leaf branch. If you let a sucker grow, it simply becomes another big stem with its own blossoms, fruits—and even its own suckers! With staked or trellised tomatoes, pinch off these suckers and just keep the energy of the plant directed at one (sometimes two or three) main stems.

If you want additional stems to develop besides the main stem, allow the suckers closest to the bottom of the plant to grow. These will have more flower blossoms and are easier to train to the outside of the plant than suckers that sprout higher up.

Tomato plants really grow fast when the weather warms up, and new suckers form all the time, so you should go on "sucker patrol" at least twice a week during the heavy growing season.

If you live in a very hot, sunny area, you can let some of the suckers put out a couple of leaves and then pinch out the tips to stop their growth. The sucker provides a little more foliage to help the plant manufacture food and also to help shade tomatoes from the sun.

Pruning Unstaked Plants

Unstaked plants can also be pruned, although it is not as necessary as it is for staked or trellised plants. Pruning improves ventilation, which can help to prevent disease problems. Pruning branches late in the season opens the plant up to more sunlight. Then on cooler days the plants are a little warmer, which is good for ripening tomatoes.

If you're growing determinate varieties of tomatoes, go easy on any pruning. Because these plants are smaller and do not continue to set new fruits throughout the season, heavy pruning may reduce your yield drastically. Also, be careful not to overprune in hot parts of the country. Tomato fruits need protection from the bright sun or they may develop sunscald. Tomatoes ripen better if they are shaded some by foliage.

Pruning Tops of Plants

You can pinch off the tip of the main stem above the top blossom of indeterminate tomato varieties to keep a flourishing plant from getting any higher. This type of pruning can be helpful when a plant is outgrowing its support, or toward the end of the growing season when a taller plant won't help much in terms of increased production. At that point, you'd prefer to see the plant put its energy into ripening the tomatoes already on the vine.

Pruning Roots

Root-pruning is a special trick you can use to speed up the ripening of early tomatoes. It simply involves cutting some of the roots of a plant when it has three or four clusters of tomatoes on it. By cutting the roots, you put quite a bit of stress on the plant, and when they're under stress, plants tend to mature more quickly. It's as if the plant were worried that it might not have time to complete its life cycle, so it rushes to mature some fruit and seed. The plant won't die if you root-prune it correctly; the growth process is simply interrupted. But after a little rest, the plant is ready to start producing again.

To root-prune trench-planted tomatoes, take a long kitchen knife and make a cut down along just one side of the buried main stem, 1 to 2 inches away from it, going down 8 to 10 inches. If the tomatoes are planted vertically, cut halfway around the plant, 1 or 2 inches from the stem, 8 to 10 inches deep. If a knife doesn't work well for you, try a spade or a shovel.

TOMATO T.L.C.

Mulching

Mulch is simply a covering over the soil that keeps moisture in, blocks weeds, and protects low-growing tomatoes from resting on the ground and developing rot. There's some extra benefit in using organic mulches such as grass clippings, hay, leaves, or sawdust because these materials—unlike plastic, aluminum, or other synthetic mulches—decompose, providing food for the millions of microorganisms that live in the soil, making nutrients available to your plants, and improving soil structure.

Mulches can raise or lower soil temperature, too. In the North, sheets of thin black plastic are often put down at planting time to warm up the soil, so that heat-loving tomatoes can get off to a good start. As soon as the sun starts hitting that plastic in the morning, the plant roots receive extra heat.

If you use a woody material as a mulch, such as bark, fresh sawdust, or wood chips, it's a good idea to add some extra nitrogen fertilizer to the soil. Otherwise the soil microorganisms, which need nitrogen for their own growth, will temporarily tie up the nitrogen your plants need until the mulch is broken down. Adding extra fertilizer supplies enough nitrogen for both plants and microorganisms. Some commercial wood mulch is pretreated with nitrogen.

In the South and Southwest, gardeners often use thick mulches of hay, straw, or pine needles to protect tomato roots from too much heat during the hot summer months, as well as to help retain moisture in the soil. Some gardeners also pile soil up 5 or 6 inches around the stems of their plants to insulate the roots more and promote some extra growth. This technique is called "hilling."

Using black plastic as mulch is good in the South and Southwest only early in the season, when the plants appreciate a little extra heat. If used in summer months, however, the roots would literally cook. It would be too hot for the plant to grow. If you use black plastic you can cover it with a heavy organic mulch that will keep soil temperature down when the weather heats up.

Some gardeners in hot areas use a commercially available mulch with an aluminum foil surface that reflects the sun and keeps the soil cool. Of course, it also keeps weeds down and conserves soil moisture.

Mulching Pointers

Many people make a big mistake by putting heavy mulches around their tomatoes too early in the season. Wait four or five weeks until the ground has really warmed up—especially in the North. With hay or any heavy mulch you are insulating the soil, so early in the season mulch keeps

the soil cool, and that's no good. You delay the harvest a few weeks if you do this.

If you're going to use black plastic, put it down at planting time when the soil is moist. (The 3-foot-wide plastic is probably best.) Secure it firmly around all the edges. The better contact the plastic makes with the soil, the more heat and moisture you trap. Then, to put in a transplant, simply punch or cut a hole or a slit in the plastic. Additional small holes here and there to let rain water soak through are a good idea, too.

Staked and trellised plants usually benefit from a mulch to save moisture. More exposed to sun and wind than unstaked plants, they lose more water through their leaves. It takes extra effort to provide them with an ample and even supply of moisture, but in dry climates, it is worth it.

Sidedressing

Tomatoes need quite a big food supply over the season —they are what we call "heavy feeders." This is no surprise when you look at all the work they're doing: extending the stem, putting out more branches, leaves, and blossoms; developing, nurturing, and ripening all those fruits! To do all this work they need a steady diet of water and nutrients.

So in most gardens, it's a good idea to sidedress tomatoes. That simply means placing fertilizer around the plants to give them extra nourishment through the season. One or two sidedressings is fine for most gardens.

Many kinds of fertilizers can give tomatoes the extra nutrients they need. Some gardeners prefer to use a complete fertilizer (such as 5-10-10 or 10-10-10). Organic fertilizers such as bone meal, dried manure, or cottonseed meal are also good. Just remember that most organic fertilizers don't contain balanced amounts of the three major nutrients—nitrogen, phosphorus, and potassium. For example, manure tends to be low in phosphorus, so you could add bone meal at the same time to provide a more complete diet.

Stay away from high nitrogen fertilizers such as urea or ammonium sulfate because it is easy to use too much. When you overfertilize, you get tall, dark-green plants with few tomatoes.

Start sidedressing when the first tomatoes have just formed—when they are about the size of golf balls. Make repeat sidedressings every three weeks after that. About a pound (2 cups) of 5-10-10 should be enough for all the plants in a 30-foot row (about twenty plants). This works out to about 1½ Tablespoons per plant spread in a 1-inch-deep circular furrow about 5 to 6 inches away from the stem, usually right under the drip line of the plant. Be careful not to get any of this fertilizer on the leaves or stem because it will burn them. Cover the fertilizer with 1 to 2 inches of soil. The next rain or watering

will start carrying the nutrients down into the root zone of the plants.

Weeds

Weeds are usually no problem around tomatoes in the home garden. As the plants are starting to grow, they are far enough apart for you to get close to do any weeding necessary. If you let some plants grow freely, you'll soon see that, with their dense foliage, they shade out weeds very well and smother them. A good mulch around staked or trellised plants will keep down weeds, so they won't rob the plants of water and nutrients.

Watering

Tomatoes like an even supply of water throughout the season; if their water supply gets turned on and off all the time they'll develop problems. We can't emphasize enough the need for an even water supply.

Like most other vegetables in the garden, tomatoes need at least 1 inch of rain or irrigation water per week for steady growth. In the hotter, dryer parts of the country, their needs go up to 2 inches of water per week during the summer months.

If you're curious about what an inch of water measures out to . . . well, it's about 60 gallons for each 100 square feet of garden. So if you ever have to water by the bucket brigade, that's something to bear in mind.

Here's a clever way of watering tomatoes. Cut the tops from some gallon-size cans, punch holes in the bottoms, and set them in the ground with only about an inch of the can showing above the surface. Use two cans near each tomato plant and fill them two or three times per week—or more often, if needed. This method directs water to the plants' root zones, and little is wasted.

You can develop your own ways of watering as long as you follow these guidelines:

Water thoroughly to encourage the tomato roots to seek water and nutrients deep in the soil. With an extensive, deep root system the plants will hold up better during dry spells. When watering, soak the soil to a depth of at least 6 to 8 inches.

Water only when your plants need it. Tomatoes like moisture, but overwatering is harmful. You not only waste water, but soggy soil will prevent the roots from getting the air they need. If your plants look a little wilted on a hot summer afternoon, that's usually normal. They'll perk up overnight. If plants are wilted in the morning, don't wait—water them! (Certain diseases can also cause wilting.) A thorough soaking every four to five days on light, sandy soils and every seven to ten days on heavy soils is a good general guide for irrigating if you don't get enough rain.

Water early in the day to cut down on evaporation losses and also to give your plants plenty of time to dry out. Wet foliage overnight may help trigger some diseases. With furrow irrigation, drip irrigation, or soaker hoses, which all deliver water right at the soil surface and not on the leaves, you can water most anytime. Try to avoid watering at midday, though, because that's when evaporation losses are highest.

Use a good mulch to help retain moisture in the soil. Mulches reduce the fluctuation of soil moisture, and that helps the crop enormously. But, remember, don't apply mulch until after the transplants have been going for five to six weeks.

COMMON TOMATO PROBLEMS

BLOSSOM END ROT

This rot begins on the bottom end of the tomato—the blossom end—as a sunken, water-soaked spot. The spot turns brown or black, dry, and leathery as it grows larger. It affects both green and ripe tomatoes and is caused by a lack of calcium in the plant that is usually the result of a fluctuating moisture supply.

Staked and pruned plants are more likely to suffer from it than unstaked tomatoes. The rot often starts when the plants are putting on some quick growth and suddenly they're hit by a hot, dry spell. They suffer moisture stress, and this brings on the problem.

Prevention is the best cure. Concentrate on keeping the water supply even throughout the season. Mulch is often a big help. It conserves soil moisture and keeps down weeds. Cultivating deeper than about an inch within a foot of the plants may damage roots and encourage rot.

One on-the-spot measure for gardeners facing a blossom end rot crisis: Apply calcium right away to the leaves. You get the calcium in the form of calcium chloride—sold by some seed companies and by hardware stores in northern areas as de-icing salt. Mix 1 tablespoon to a gallon of water and spray two or three times a week. This will help some.

CRACKING

Tomatoes often start to crack during warm, rainy periods—especially if this weather comes after a dry spell. The tomatoes simply expand too fast. They are most likely to crack when they have reached full size and are beginning to turn color. Some varieties are resistant to cracking, such as *Early Girl*, *Heinz 1350*, and *Jet Star*. Again, the best way to avoid the problem is to keep the moisture supply as steady as possible throughout the season.

CATFACING

This is another kind of cracking or scarring. Tomatoes develop unusual swelling and streaks of scar tissue. It is not a disease; it is caused by abnormal development of the tomato flower at blossom time. Cool weather is believed to cause the flower problems.

BLOSSOM DROP

Some years many of the early-season blooms simply fall off without setting fruit. This is the result of cool night temperatures (below 55°F). Some varieties such as *Pixie* will keep their blossoms and set fruit in cool weather. Blossom drop also occurs when day temperatures are consistently above 90°F or night temperatures remain above 75°F in the summer. This is one of the reasons why it is often difficult to get a summer-long crop of tomatoes in the hot sections of the South and Southwest. Certain varieties, such as *Homestead 24*, will set fruits well even under hot, dry conditions.

CURLING OF LEAVES

Curling or "leaf roll" is very common but does not harm production. It usually occurs after periods of heavy rains, when the soil is very wet. Older leaves are affected, rolling up until their edges touch. Some varieties are more prone to leaf roll than others. Plant in well-drained soil to minimize leaf roll.

SUNSCALD

This occurs when green or ripening tomatoes get too much exposure to the hot sun. At first, a yellowish-white patch appears on the side of the tomato facing the sun. The area gets larger as the fruit ripens and becomes grayish-white. To guard against sunscald, be careful not to overprune and remove foliage shading the fruits. Especially in hot climates, it may be a good idea to grow plants in cages where they'll develop lots of protective foliage. Control diseases such as early blight that cause plants to lose foliage.

Although these common problems make tomatoes look ugly, they're okay to eat fresh. Just cut away the affected part and enjoy the rest.

Insects

Let's run down some of the more common tomato insect problems gardeners have to deal with from time to time. For more information on the pests that are most likely to cause problems in your part of the country and how to control them, contact your local county extension agent.

Aphids can bother tomato plants all season long. These soft-bodied, pear-shaped insects may be green, pink, or yellow. They suck the sap from plants, weakening them, and, indirectly, spread diseases. To control, spray with an approved insecticide.

Blister beetles and Colorado potato beetles both feed

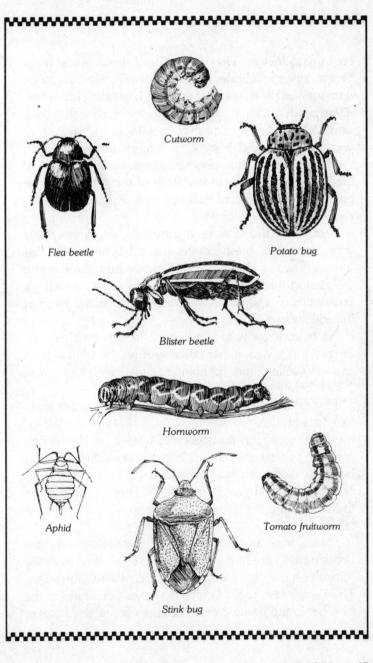

Cutworm

Flea beetle

Potato bug

Blister beetle

Hornworm

Aphid

Stink bug

Tomato fruitworm

on tomato foliage. The ½- to ¾-inch-long, black, gray, brown, or yellow blister beetles generally don't do much damage. Just keep an eye out when harvesting tomatoes; if you crush one of these beetles, its juices can cause your skin to blister. The Colorado potato beetle is a more voracious feeder. Adult beetles are orange and black striped; the large, orange, humpbacked larvae have two rows of black dots down their sides. Both of these pests can be controlled with diligent hand-picking. Approved insecticides will also give control.

Cutworms: If you've seen cutworms, you know these gray, brown, or black critters curl up tightly when disturbed. They're about 1 to 1½ inches long, hide in the soil during the day, and come out at night to feed on young plants. They'll chew tomato transplants right off at the soil surface.

No need to spray for these pests in the home garden. Simply put a newspaper collar around the tender stem at transplanting time, spanning at least 1 inch above and 1 inch below ground (see page 20).

Flea beetles: These tiny, ⅟₁₆-inch black beetles jump like fleas and chew numerous small holes in the leaves, most often early in the season. Damage on established plants is usually not serious, but young seedlings can be badly weakened by flea beetle damage. To control, spray or dust with an approved insecticide. Adult beetles spend the winter in plant debris, so clean up the garden in the fall.

Hornworms are probably many gardeners' least favorite pest. These huge, green caterpillars with a thornlike "horn" on their back end eat both leaves and tomatoes. They work fast, too. Handpicking these creatures is the best bet in the home garden because you often discover them at harvest time when it is unwise to spray with chemical insecticides. (The "horn" is fierce-looking, but harmless.) A natural insecticide which requires no waiting between application and harvest is *Bacillus thuringiensis* (available as Dipel or Thuricide). This causes a disease that infects only caterpillars. It is most effective if used when the caterpillars are small.

Stinkbugs are mainly a problem in the southern part of the country. These ⅝-inch-long, shield-shaped insects may be green, gray, blue, or red. Like aphids, they feed by sucking the plants' sap. This causes deformed fruits with hard, whitish spots on them. To control these pests, keep down nearby weeds that may harbor them and spray with an approved insecticide.

Tomato fruitworm is a season-long pest that feeds on tomato foliage and fruits. These yellow, green, or brown striped caterpillars get up to 2 inches long. Spray with an approved insecticide for control. Destroy infested fruits and clean up all tomato plant debris at the end of the season to reduce the number of overwintering insects.

Whiteflies will feed on many plants in the vegetable garden besides tomatoes, including cucumbers and melons. These tiny (1/16-inch-long) pests fly out in a cloud from infested plants when disturbed. They feed by sucking the plants' sap, causing leaves to become yellow and distorted, and weakening plants. Whiteflies secrete a sugary substance called honeydew on which a sooty black mold often grows, making tomato leaves appear dirty. Spray with an approved insecticide for control.

If you use chemical sprays, be very careful about following the directions exactly. Read the directions three times: (1) before you make a purchase, so you know what you are getting; (2) before you use it, to make sure you use it correctly; and (3) after you have used it, so that you store it properly, out of risk to people and pets.

Diseases

Early blight, a fungus disease, is a common problem east of the Mississippi and in the far West. The first signs of trouble appear on the lower leaves as small brown spots with concentric rings in their centers and yellow margins. Affected leaves eventually turn yellow and fall from the plant. Fruits may also be affected. Warm, humid weather favors the spread of this disease.

To help keep early blight in check, clean up all tomato plant remains at the end of the season, since disease-causing spores can survive over the winter on plant debris. Mulch plants to reduce splashing spore-carrying soil onto leaves during rains, avoid wetting the foliage when you water, and make sure there is good air circulation around plants by not crowding them.

There are chemical fungicide sprays that can control early blight if applied regularly when weather conditions are favorable for the spread of the disease. Check with your local county extension agent to find out what fungicides are recommended in your state. Be sure you read the label and follow all the directions carefully when using any pesticide.

Late blight is another fungus disease that affects tomatoes in the same geographical areas as early blight. Leaves develop bluish-gray spots, then turn brown and drop. Fruits develop dark-brown, corky spots. Wet weather with warm days and cool nights sets the stage for this disease, which also infects potatoes.

To control late blight, clean up tomato plant debris in

the garden at the end of the season, avoid wetting the foliage when you water, and use an approved fungicide regularly.

Leaf spot can be caused by several different kinds of fungi. It is often a problem in the southeastern states and some northern areas that have warm, moist weather. Septoria leaf spot is common in the northeastern, mid-Atlantic, and central states, while gray leaf spot is common in the Southeast. Septoria begins with many small brown spots with black specks in their centers; older leaves are affected first. Eventually infected leaves turn yellow and drop. Gray leaf spot is similar, except that the spots have gray centers.

The fungi that cause these diseases live on old tomato plant debris in the soil and nearby perennial weeds. Rotating crops from one spot to another in the garden each year is one way to keep this disease in check. Clean up the garden well at the end of the season, avoid overhead watering, and apply an approved fungicide regularly.

Notes on Disease Prevention

Rotate your crop of tomatoes each year to avoid soil-borne diseases. Some serious diseases can live in the soil for several years. Try to wait three years before planting tomatoes where they grew before. Also, avoid planting where potatoes or eggplants grew the previous season, since some diseases attack all these vegetables and live in the soil from year to year.

Plant resistant varieties. Many tomato varieties are resistant to verticillium wilt and fusarium wilt, two troublesome diseases for which there is no cure. Fusarium causes yellowing of the leaves, wilting, and early death of the plant. Verticillium causes similar symptoms, but seldom kills tomato plants. Growth slows down, plants lose leaves, and fruits may develop sunscald because of poor foliage cover.

Many seed companies list resistance to these diseases by putting "F" (Fusarium) or "V" (Verticillium) after the variety name. "N" stands for resistance to nematodes, the tiny worms that plague many southern gardens, causing stunting of the plants and poor crops.

Don't let anyone smoke in the garden since they can infect plants with tobacco mosaic virus, a serious disease that can really cut down on the harvest. If you smoke, wash your hands with soap and water before handling tomato plants.

Clean up the garden well at the end of the season. Many disease-causing organisms spend the winter in plant debris in the soil. Destroy any obviously infected plant material rather than composting it.

Help is available if you need it. Remember that your local county extension service can help you identify diseases and recommend remedies. Many offices publish pamphlets with pictures and descriptions of tomato plant problems you may encounter in your part of the country.

The Great Tomato Race

To have the first ripe tomato in your neighborhood:

Select an early variety—such as *Pixie, Stokes Alaska,* or other tomato known to set fruit well in cool weather.

Plant the seeds yourself indoors ten to twelve weeks or more before the average last spring frost date.

Repot the seedlings into a deep container when they are 3 or 4 inches high, picking off all the lower leaves and putting the plant in up to the leaves. Repot a second time when the plants are 8 to 10 inches high, again pinching off all the lower leaves and setting the plants as deep in tall milk cartons or pots as you can.

Harden off the plants well—at least for ten days. You should try to get the plants in the ground two or three weeks before the average last frost date, so plan your hardening period accordingly.

Choose a sunny section of the garden for your tomatoes. Till or spade the soil there deep, mixing in a generous amount of fetilizer, compost, or manure. If possible, transplant on a cloudy day. In sunny weather, try to wait until late afternoon or evening.

If you transplant according to the trench method, the roots will be near the surface. If you set the plant in the ground vertically, keep the roots close to the surface by not planting them deeper than before, so they can warm up. Soak the area after transplanting. Don't use any mulch except black plastic.

Use some kind of heat-gathering technique—such as hotcaps or circling the plants with black felt roofing paper or with an old tire. The more heat you draw to the plant, the sooner the harvest.

It's vital to use windbreaks and frost-protection devices such as hotcaps, paper bags, or bushel baskets.

Spray flower clusters twice a week with "blossom set," a hormone spray which helps fruit setting.

Sidedress the plants with a balanced fertilizer when the plant has blossomed.

Be sure the plants get enough water and watch out for signs of insect or disease damage.

Root-prune a couple of tomato plants when they have formed three or four clusters of tomatoes. This will hasten ripening.

Before harvesting your first vine-ripened tomato—weeks before your neighbors—ask them over to witness the event and collect your bets right on the spot!

Tomatoes in Crocks, Pots, and Baskets

Tomatoes will surprise you! They can stand mighty close quarters and still deliver. So if you have a hanging planter or a bushel basket and a sunny spot somewhere, you can grow your own!

Some points to keep in mind:

Sun. Container tomatoes, like those in the garden, need at least six to eight hours of sunshine a day to produce a worthwhile harvest. If you grow them indoors, put them where they'll get maximum sunshine . . . moving the container from window to window if you must.

Soil. For hanging planters and small pots, regular potting soil is good. With larger containers, you may want to use a lighter weight, soilless growing mix, such as Jiffy-Mix or Pro-Mix. It will retain moisture very well, which is important for tomatoes. Garden soil is okay to use, but needs to be lightened with peat moss, vermiculite, or perlite, to improve its drainage.

Containers. Almost anything will do. You can have a great crop from a plant in a 5-gallon can or pot, a smaller hanging planter . . . or even a bushel basket. Just be sure that whatever container you choose has holes in the bottom for drainage.

To plant in bushel baskets, line them with plastic bags to keep the dirt in and retain moisture. Put an inch of stones at the bottom of the bags and poke through some drainage holes. Three tomato plants in a basket, supported by short stakes, look beautiful on a deck.

Varieties. Cherry tomatoes and other small varieties are the ones to grow in containers. If you're trying container growing for the first time, a cherry patio type such as *Sweet 100*, *Tiny Tim*, or *Pixie* is a good choice. They are easy to support (or you can let them trail from a hanging container) and they'll produce very early.

Water. Container tomatoes need watering often because the plant roots obviously can't reach for extra moisture as garden tomatoes do. In the heat of the summer when the plants are big, water them daily.

Fertilizer. Give the plants some fertilizer every week or so. Mix a small amount of soluble balanced fertilizer into their water. Tomatoes like regular feedings of small amounts of fertilizer rather than infrequent, large doses.

Planting. Pinch off the lower leaves of the seedlings and set them in the baskets, pots, or hanging planters vertically as deep as you can. For fall pot plantings, take 6- to 8-inch suckers or "slips" from tomato plants in the garden (smaller varieties preferred), set them in a deep pot, and water heavily for a day or two. When you bring these pots or baskets indoors and give them a sunny home, you can extend the tomato harvest for many weeks.

Pollination. When the plants have flowered, give them a little shake in the middle of the day to help pollination along.

Care. Whether they're on the back porch or in the house, tomatoes need protection from insects and diseases just like garden plants.

HARVESTING

One of the great joys of gardening is reaching for the first red-ripe tomato on the vine and biting into it. There's a flavor, juiciness, and pleasure you'll never get from a supermarket tomato. Because tomatoes ripen from the inside out, when the outer skin is firm and red, you know you've got a beautiful ripe one.

The red color of tomatoes won't form when the temperatures are above 86°F. So if you live where the summers get quite hot, leaving tomatoes on the vine may give them a yellowish-orange look. It's probably better to pick them in the pink stage and let them ripen indoors in cooler temperatures.

Tomatoes don't need light to ripen, so don't put them on a sunny windowsill. Put them in a place out of direct sunlight—even in a dark cupboard—where the temperature is around 65 or 70°F.

Frost-Time Harvest

Tomatoes will succumb to the lightest frost, but don't panic when the weatherman predicts the first frost and your tomato vines are still loaded with green fruit. If it's going to be a light frost, you can protect the plants overnight by covering them with old sheets, plastic, burlap bags, or big boxes. It's usually worth the effort because the second frost is often two or three weeks after the first one.

If a heavy freeze is on its way, go out and pick all the tomatoes. Green tomatoes that have reached about three-fourths of their full size will eventually ripen, and smaller, immature green ones can be pickled.

Some people like to pull up the whole tomato plant and hang it upside down in a dark basement room and let the tomatoes ripen gradually. You just have to check them regularly to keep a very ripe tomato from falling onto the floor—*splaat!*

Another method is to put all the tomatoes that need ripening on a shelf and cover them with sheets of newspaper. Some people wrap up each tomato individually, but that's too much work—especially when you want to check for ripe tomatoes. You have to open each one! Instead, you can just lift up the flat newspaper cover, take a peek, and take all the ripe tomatoes and remove any that may have started to rot. The newspaper covering

helps trap a natural ethylene gas that tomatoes give off which hastens ripening.

Fall Tomatoes

In parts of the southern and southwestern states you can grow an abundant crop of fall tomatoes.

The big question is, "Where do I buy young tomato plants in the middle of the summer?" It's often hard to find them for sale.

An easy way to solve the problem is to cut small suckers from spring-planted tomatoes and let them grow to full-sized plants. Instead of pinching out most of the suckers on your tomato plants, allow some to grow 4 or 5 inches and produce a bud. Then in mid or late summer, cut the suckers from the plant, remove the lower leaves up to the bud, and set them in a jar of water for an hour or two. This will start the rooting process. Then plant them in pots or directly in the garden. Firm the soil around the suckers and water them heavily for two or three days.

You can also simply lop off the top foot or so of a healthy plant and set it in water and plant it later.

These plants will do just as well as any you could raise from scratch or buy at a garden store. They'll give you a nice fall crop, too.

PRESERVING YOUR HARVEST

Tomatoes are wonderful!

They taste best fresh from the garden with the warmth of the sun still in them, but also go great in salads, broiled, baked, fried, with eggs or cheese, as relish, in stews, stuffed—fantastic both summer and winter.

Cherry tomatoes are great as appetizers; Italian plum tomatoes are especially good for sauces and cooking. Beefsteak tomatoes—the really nice, big, fat, firm ones —are terrific for slicing or stuffing. And the "garden variety" tomatoes are excellent broiled, served plain, in salads, or canned whole or stewed.

Tomatoes come in such pretty colors, too—luscious golds and yellows—but for us nothing beats a beautiful red one.

Until the beginning of this century, in many areas of this country, people didn't eat tomatoes because they thought they were poisonous. The green leaves really are toxic (tomatoes are related to other noxious plants such as deadly nightshade, belladonna, and tobacco); but we know that the fruit of the tomato plant makes for fine eating!

CANNING TOMATOES

It's satisfying to see jars of tomatoes in neat rows on the pantry shelf, but the real benefit comes in the eating. In winter when the stores carry only mealy, dry, flavorless, pale pink things they call tomatoes, you can turn to your own storehouse of home-grown and home-canned ones for a real taste treat.

Boiling Water Bath Canning

1. *For safety, it is always important to use careful canning techniques.* Because tomatoes contain sufficient acid, they may be canned safely in a boiling water bath* rather than in a pressure canner as required for all other vegetables. *If you are canning tomato sauce that contains meat or other vegetables, use the pressure canning method.*

  Because instructions accompanying canners sometimes vary, follow the instructions that came with yours.

2. *Assemble all utensils:* canner with rack, Mason jars, lids, tongs or jar lifter, timer, cooling racks, wide-mouth funnel, slotted spoon, nonmetallic spatula.

Use only Mason jars for home canning; they are made by a number of manufacturers. These jars are safe for canning because the glass is heat-tempered, and they can seal perfectly.

Never reuse dome lids for canning. The rubber compound loses its ability to seal perfectly after one use. Metal screw bands and Mason jars may be reused.

3. *Examine and clean all equipment.* Check all bands for rust, dents, or nicks and the jars for chips or cracks. Recycle them or use them in the workshop or elsewhere if they are not perfect.

Wash all equipment in hot, soapy water. Rinse in clear, hot water. Keep jars and screw tops hot. Follow manufacturer's directions for preparing the metal lids.

4. *Use the freshest, cleanest tomatoes possible. One bushel of tomatoes will yield about 18 quarts of tomatoes; 3 pounds of tomatoes will produce 1 quart.* Of course, if you cook them down for sauce, paste, or juice, the yield varies.

Wash tomatoes well.

To peel them, put them in boiling water for thirty seconds until the skin splits. Put them in cold water briefly.

---

*If you have any questions about basic canning methods, your local county extension service can provide lots of helpful information. They generally have free or low-cost publications with the latest recommendations on home food preservation.

You may also wish to send for the USDA Bulletin No. 8, *Home Canning of Fruits and Vegetables*, if it is not available from your local extension office. Write or call for current price information: Government Printing Office, Publications Service Section, STOP SSOS, Washington, D.C. 20240, (202)275-3050.

Then you can slip the skins off easily with a paring knife.

Remove the stems and any green spots from the tomatoes, and do not use any tomatoes that are overripe or unhealthy. One bad tomato is like one bad apple—it can spoil the whole batch. So, be careful when you select your tomatoes.

Tomatoes don't always have to be peeled. If they are going to be used in smooth sauce or in juice, there's no need to peel them. When they are sieved or strained, the skins will be eliminated.

5. *Hot pack:* In a large pot, bring tomatoes (whole or chopped) to a boil in their own juice. Boil for five minutes, stirring constantly. Pour the hot tomatoes into hot jars, leaving ½ inch headspace. Release all air bubbles from the jar by running a clean spatula down around the inside of the jar. Wipe jar top and threads with a clean, damp cloth. Put lid, rubber side down, on jar and screw band on firmly.

Cold pack: This method, in which unheated tomatoes are packed into jars, then processed, is no longer recommended by the USDA for reasons of both quality and safety.

In recent years there has been concern about low-acid

tomatoes. Most garden varieties of tomatoes are not low-acid. However, if you feel your tomatoes may be a low-acid variety, you may add 2 Tablespoons *bottled* lemon juice or ½ teaspoon citric acid per quart of tomatoes.

6. *Process in water-bath canner.* Fill the canner half full with hot—not boiling—water. Place rack in bottom. Put filled jars in canner, so that they do not touch each other or the side of the pot. Add hot water, if necessary, so that the jars are covered with at least 1 to 2 inches of water. Cover. Start timing when water reaches a rolling boil.

CANNING TIMES

	Headspace	Jar Size	Boiling Time
Paste	¼ inch	½ pint/pint	45 minutes
Plain puree	¼ inch	½ pint/pint	30 minutes
Seasoned puree	¼ inch	½ pint/pint	45 minutes
Whole tomatoes			
Hot pack	½ inch	pint	35 minutes
	½ inch	quart	45 minutes
Juice	¼ inch	pint	35 minutes
	¼ inch	quart	35 minutes

Do not skimp on processing time. This is very important to ensure that all bacteria are killed. Altitude lowers the temperature at which water boils, so increase processing time two minutes for each 1,000 feet above sea level.

7. *Complete the processing.* Using tongs or jar lifter, remove the jars and put them upright on a rack or thick towel in a draft-free area, allowing enough room between jars so that air may circulate freely.

Do not tighten the metal rims, because you may break the seals.

8. *After twelve to twenty-four hours test the seal.* As the jar cools, contraction of the contents during cooling

will pull and firmly attach the self-sealing lid and form a high vacuum. When this happens you often hear a "click" or "kerplunking" sound.

The lid will be concave or dished, which means the jar is sealed properly. If you can push the center down with your thumb the seal is *not* complete.

If you find some jars with incomplete seals you have several choices. You may put the jars in the refrigerator and use the food right away; you may freeze the tomatoes if you have freezer space; or you may reprocess tomatoes within *twenty-four hours*. If you do reprocess, put on new lids and process the full time. This will result in mushier tomatoes but will be perfectly safe.

9. *Remove the metal rings before storing.* They serve no purpose once the jar is sealed and you can use them over many times. Wipe the jars with a clean, damp cloth, label, and store in a cool, dry, dark place.

10. *Before serving, reheat canned tomatoes.* To be on the safe side, it is recommended that you simmer stewed tomatoes or sauce for ten to fifteen minutes—without tasting—to make sure any bacteria are killed. If the tomatoes smell "off" or if the color or appearance doesn't look right, don't taste them. Throw them out so that even pets or wild animals can't get at them. Rule of

thumb: When in doubt, throw it out!

If you follow these easy steps, you can have lots of good eating!

TOMATO JUICE

Cut washed, cored, and unpeeled tomatoes into quarters and cook slowly in a large, heavy stainless or enamel pot until the tomatoes are soft. Press them through a food mill or strainer. Salt, sugar, and spices may be added, if desired. After straining, reheat juice until it is almost boiling. Pour it hot into the jars, leaving ¼ inch headspace. Wipe jar tops and threads clean. Put lid, rubber side down, on jar, and screw band on firmly. Process in a boiling water bath for thirty-five minutes for both pints and quarts.

TOMATO SAUCE

Use whatever recipe you like; a good one is on page 66. Just remember that if the recipe calls for meat or any vegetables other than tomatoes, you will need to process the sauce in a pressure canner or freeze it. (It is not safe to can vegetables other than tomatoes in a boiling water bath because they are not acid enough.) For mixtures of vegetables, pressure process according to the recommendations for the vegetable in the mixture needing the longest processing.

TOMATO PASTE

Try the recipe on page 69. It's good, but all tomato pastes take so many tomatoes and such a lot of time to cook down, you may decide they're not worth the energy consumption for home processing.

FREEZING TOMATOES

Whether it's practical for you to freeze tomatoes or tomato sauce depends on the size of your freezer and what else you need to store in it. Because tomatoes can so well, you may want to save your freezer space for other things.

Freezing sauce is handy, especially if you have just a pint or two left over from a whole canning batch or if you want to add meat or other vegetables to part of a batch of tomato sauce and don't want to drag out the pressure canner. Just put the sauce in containers, leaving ½-inch headspace, and put them in the freezer.

In the summer when tomatoes are ripe, you may not have much time. To make time, simply stew cored tomatoes after washing them. Cook them down slowly, adding just a little sugar. Then freeze the plain, cooked-down tomatoes in pint containers. In the winter you'll have a freezer full of garden tomatoes ready for sauces and stews with a minimum of hassle.

Yes, you can freeze whole tomatoes! Whole tomatoes, which have been scalded for thirty seconds in boiling water—just enough time to loosen their skins—may be frozen raw and whole. This is especially handy if you have an oversupply, but select especially meaty ones for freezing whole, because otherwise they break down and are fairly mushy when thawed.

Place the tomatoes, whole or sliced, on a greased cookie sheet; put it in the freezer. After twenty-four hours, when the tomatoes are frozen solid, place them in containers.

FAVORITE RECIPES

TOMATO SAUCE

A few batches of this sauce should last a family of four all winter and spring. Use for spaghetti, lasagna, veal and eggplant parmesan, goulash, stew, soups, and many different casseroles.

1 peck (12–15 pounds) fresh tomatoes
2 cups chopped onion
1 cup chopped green pepper
1 cup chopped celery
2 Tbsp brown sugar
2 cloves garlic, finely minced
1 Tbsp parsley, minced
1 Tbsp basil
1 Tbsp oregano
1½ Tbsp plain (noniodized) salt (optional)
½ tsp pepper

Wash ripe tomatoes well and, if you want to peel them, dip in boiling water briefly until the skins split. Rinse in cold water. Remove cores and green spots. To reduce cooking time, chop tomatoes. Put in a large, heavy kettle. It is important to use a heavy pan so that the tomatoes do not stick or scorch.

Simmer the tomatoes two hours, stirring frequently. Add the remaining ingredients and, using an asbestos pad on the stove burner, simmer overnight or until the sauce has cooked down by half.

You can also cook the tomato sauce down in the oven.

Fill a large roasting pan with prepared tomatoes, set in the oven at 250°F, and let it cook until it's as thick as you want it. Stir occasionally as it cooks. With this method, there's no danger of burning the sauce, and it doesn't take up space on the top of the stove.

If you want a smooth sauce, or if you haven't peeled the tomatoes, you may sieve the sauce or run it through a blender or food processor.

Pour hot sauce into hot jars, leaving ¼ inch headspace. Adjust lids. Process in a pressure canner with 10 lbs. pressure, twenty minutes for pints, twenty-five minutes for quarts. Makes 8 pints.

What if you don't have a pressure canner? You can still make tomato sauce, but you'll need to make some changes. The above recipe contains low-acid vegetables (onions, peppers, and celery) that make it unsafe to process except in a pressure canner. But, if you omit the low-acid vegetables, using only the tomatoes, sugar, garlic, herbs, and spices in the above recipe, you can safely process the sauce in a boiling water bath for forty-five minutes.

Another alternative is to include the low-acid vegetables when making the sauce, but freeze it instead of canning it.

Below are some of the easy and interesting ways this basic sauce can be changed to create really different tastes. The proportions are based on 1 quart of sauce. *These ingredients are added when preparing the sauce for a meal—not prior to canning.* Some of these additions would necessitate pressure canning and/or drastically lengthen the processing time if added prior to canning.

Prior to serving, if the sauce is too thick, add beef consommé, stock, or red or white wine to thin it to the consistency you like.

Three slices of bacon, sautéed and crumbled, ½ lb of browned, lean ground beef, ½ to 1 lb sliced, sauteed mushrooms, ¼ cup grated cheese (cheddar, Parmesan, or whatever you have on hand).

One-quarter cup browned, minced lean ham, 1 cup browned, chopped beef, 1 strip of lemon peel, pinch of nutmeg, 1 cup of beef stock, ½ cup dry white wine. Before serving, remove lemon peel and add ¼ cup of whipping cream.

Half-pound browned sausage, ½ lb browned ground beef, 4 or 5 crushed mint leaves.

Half-pound ground, browned lamb, 3 bay leaves, ½ cup dry white or red wine.

Tiny meatballs made of 1 cup soft breadcrumbs, 1 Tbsp milk, ½ lb ground beef, parsley, 1 egg. Brown them well under the broiler or in a skillet before adding them to the basic sauce.

One ounce boned anchovies; small can of tuna; 6 large, pitted, chopped, black olives; ¾ cup diced mozzarella cheese.

Small pinches of saffron, coriander, fennel, and basil, 1-inch piece of dried orange peel.

TOMATO PASTE

6 quarts Italian tomatoes
1 Tbsp salt (optional)

In a heavy enamel, stainless, or aluminum pot, cook tomatoes with salt, if desired, until soft. When soft, put through food mill, fine sieve, or food processor and re-heat. Simmer using an asbestos mat. It is most important to prevent scorching—stirring frequently helps. After several hours the pulp will be reduced to a thick paste. Pack hot in hot, half-pint jars, leaving ¼ inch headspace. Release air bubbles, adjust lids, and water bath process forty-five minutes.

To make handy pasteballs you can spread the paste on moist plates to a depth of ½ inch. You may then dry it in the sun or in a warm oven. When it's dry enough, roll the paste into balls and dip them in olive oil. They can then be stored in an airtight jar in the refrigerator.

POTTSFIELD PICKLE

A *good way to use leftover tomatoes—both red and green—at the end of the season.*

3 pints green tomatoes
3 pints firm, red tomatoes
3 large onions
3 sweet red peppers
3 bunches of celery (or less)
½ cup salt (noniodized)
1 tsp cinnamon
1 tsp cloves
½ cup white mustard seed
3 pints vinegar
4 cups sugar

Cut up all the vegetables; add salt. Let the mixture sit for six hours or overnight. Drain and rinse. Add spices, vinegar, and sugar; cook until tender. It will be juicy. Pour in hot, sterile jars, leaving ¼ inch headspace. Adjust lids and process for fifteen minutes in boiling water bath. Makes 6 to 8 pints.

TOMATO APPLE CHUTNEY

20 medium, ripe tomatoes
 8 apples
 3 large onions
 2 large, sweet red or green peppers
 1 hot red pepper
 1 cup seedless raisins
2½ cups brown sugar
 1 clove garlic, crushed
 2 tsp each ground ginger, cinnamon
 1 tsp salt
3½ cups vinegar

Scald tomatoes in boiling water, cool, and peel. Pare apples. Peel onions. Core peppers. Chop all roughly. Combine all ingredients and simmer in heavy, covered kettle for about two hours or until mixture is thick. Stir frequently to prevent sticking. Pour boiling hot into hot, sterile jars. Leave ¼ inch headspace. Process ten minutes in boiling water bath.

TOMATO JAM

1 lb tomatoes, red, green, or yellow
1 lb sugar
  grated rind of 1 lemon or orange
2 ounces ginger root or preserved ginger
1 4-inch cinnamon stick

Peel, core, and slice tomatoes. Cover with sugar and let stand for twelve hours. Strain off the juice and boil it until the syrup falls from the spoon in heavy drops. Add the tomatoes, rind, and spices. Cook until jam thickens and then put in hot, sterile jars. Process in a boiling water bath for five minutes.

SPICY TOMATO RELISH

Serve this with meats instead of store-bought ketchup.

20 tomatoes, peeled and chopped
1½ cups chopped onion
 1 cup chopped green pepper
1¼ cup sugar, white or brown
 2 tsp celery seed
 2 tsp plain (noniodized) salt
 ¾ tsp each cinnamon, cloves, ginger, allspice
 1 cup vinegar

Mix all ingredients in a large, heavy kettle. Bring to boil and then simmer until as thick as desired. Stir to prevent sticking. Pour, boiling hot, into hot jars. Leave ¼ inch headspace and adjust lids. Process ten minutes in boiling water bath. Makes about 8 pints.

FRESH SLICED TOMATOES...

... a sprinkling of oil, fresh chopped basil, salt, and pepper
... raw spinach, onions, and anchovies
... cucumbers, dill, oil, and vinegar
... a sprinkling of oil, a dash of vinegar, chopped onions, and oregano
... mayonnaise
... in a sandwich with lettuce, bacon, and cheese
... sour cream and chives

NO-POT TOMATOES

Serve these with grilled hamburgers, steak, or chicken for an easy No-Pot-Supper.

Per Serving:
 1 tomato
 ½ onion
 ½ tsp olive oil or butter
  salt and pepper
  pinch of basil, tarragon, and oregano
  sprinkle of garlic salt

    Wash, core, and cut each tomato into eight chunks. Peel the onions, chop them roughly, and add to tomatoes. Add butter or oil, salt, pepper, and herbs. Wrap the mixture in foil and seal the edges well. (You may even want to wrap it in two layers.) Tuck the package down in the coals or place it on the grill. Depending on the heat of the fire, allow fifteen to thirty minutes, enough time for the onions to get tender.

STUFFED TOMATOES

6 firm, red tomatoes, 3 to 4 inches in diameter
½ lb sausage meat or lean, chopped beef
1 medium onion, finely chopped
¾ cup rice
 olive oil
1 clove garlic, minced
1 tsp finely chopped fresh basil
1 tsp finely chopped fresh parsley
 salt and pepper to taste
4 Tbsp Parmesan cheese

Cut tops off unpeeled, washed tomatoes. Save the tops. Squeeze or scoop out the seeds of the tomatoes and reserve the juice. Sprinkle insides with salt and invert to drain.

Brown meat, drain fat, and set aside. Sauté onion and rice in olive oil in heavy skillet over medium heat until rice is translucent and just turning golden. Combine meat, rice, herbs, cheese, and reserved tomato juice.

Stuff shells with mixture. Because the rice swells in cooking, fill the shells only half full. Place tomatoes on oiled, shallow baking pan and bake in preheated 350° oven for fifty minutes or until tomatoes are soft but still firm. May be served hot or cold.

SCALLOPED TOMATOES

¼ cup chopped onion
¼ cup chopped green pepper
¼ cup margarine
6 cups tomatoes, peeled and cut up, fresh or canned
  salt and pepper to taste
1 Tbsp sugar
1½ cups toasted bread cubes

Cook onion and green pepper in margarine until tender. In a 2-quart casserole, mix all ingredients together, except for ½ cup bread cubes. Sprinkle top with remaining bread cubes and bake in preheated 350° oven for thirty minutes. Serves 6. For even better taste, top with grated cheese and put under broiler until bubbly brown.

BAKED/BROILED TOMATOES

These are an easy, delicious addition for brunch, lunch, or supper that makes guests think you've gone to a lot of trouble.

Per Serving:
 1 **tomato**
   salt and pepper
   pinches of basil, oregano
½ **ounce grated cheese**
½ **slice of bacon**
   bread crumbs
   pat of butter

Wash tomatoes and core. Cut in half crosswise and sprinkle with salt and pepper, herbs, and top with cheese, bacon, bread crumbs, and butter. Put on oiled baking pan and bake in preheated 400° oven fifteen minutes or until tomatoes are tender but not soft. Put under broiler for a minute to brown.

TOMATO BREAD

This *unusual, reddish bread is wonderful as a base for*
melted cheese sandwiches and mini-pizzas.

- **2 cups tomato juice**
- **2 Tbsp butter**
- **3 Tbsp sugar**
- **1 tsp salt**
- **½ tsp each basil, oregano**
- **¼ cup ketchup**
- **¼ cup grated cheese**
- **1 pkg active dry yeast**
- **¼ cup warm water (110° to 115° F)**
- **7 cups sifted, all-purpose flour**

Heat tomato juice and butter together until the butter
is melted. Add sugar, salt, herbs, ketchup, and cheese,
and let mixture cool to lukewarm. Sprinkle yeast on warm
water and stir to dissolve. Add tomato mixture and 3 cups
of flour to yeast. Beat with electric mixer at medium speed,
scraping the bowl occasionally. Mix for two minutes or
beat by hand until smooth.

Gradually mix in enough remaining flour to make soft
dough that leaves the side of the bowl. Turn onto lightly
floured board and knead for eight to ten minutes, when
dough will be elastic and smooth. Place in lightly greased
bowl; turn dough over so top is greased.

Cover and let rise in warm place until doubled—1 to
1½ hours. Punch down and divide in half. Cover and let
rest ten minutes. Shape into loaves and place in greased,
9 × 5 × 3″ loaf pans. Cover and let rise until almost

doubled, about one hour.

Bake in hot oven (375°F) about twenty-five minutes or until done. Makes 2 loaves.

FRIED TOMATOES

Core and slice tomatoes; they can be either green or red. Dip the slices in flour to which some salt and sugar have been added. Brown slices on both sides in butter or bacon fat (bacon fat is better) until crisp. Turn just once. When brown on both sides, put the slices in a casserole in a warm oven. Some of the browning flour will remain in the skillet, and that's okay. Just add more butter or fat as needed for browning more slices.

When all the slices are done, add milk gradually to the pan, stirring constantly over a moderate heat to make gravy. Season as needed. Pour hot sauce over tomatoes and serve promptly. If you don't, the tomatoes will get soggy.

CANDIED CHERRY TOMATOES

¼ cup chopped onion
3 Tbsp butter
4 cups cherry tomatoes
½ cup brown sugar or honey
¾ tsp salt
1½ cup buttered bread crumbs

Sauté onion in butter. Add washed cherry tomatoes with stems removed, 6 Tbsp of brown sugar or honey, and salt. Cook very slowly, using asbestos mat under skillet to prevent sticking, until liquid evaporates. Put mixture in baking dish. Top with bread crumbs and remaining sugar or honey and bake in 350° oven until crumbs are brown.

Another way to serve cherry tomatoes is sautéed in butter with garlic, chives, dill, or shallots. Or leave their stems on and dunk them raw in sour cream and chives.

SORT-OF-SPANISH RICE

¼ cup chopped onion
3 Tbsp chopped green pepper
1 cup raw rice
2 Tablespoons oil
2 tsp sugar
2 cups stewed tomatoes
4 pork chops or ¾ lb hot sausage
½ cup grated Parmesan cheese

Sauté onion, green pepper, and rice in oil until rice is translucent. Add sugar and tomatoes to skillet. Top with pork chops and cheese. Bake, covered, in 350°F oven for about one hour. Serves 4. Served with a green salad, it's a one-pot supper even kids can prepare.

GAZPACHO (OR SALAD SOUP)

2 cloves garlic
2 slices white bread
1 sliced cucumber
½ chopped green pepper
½ cup water
¼ cup olive oil
2 lbs ripe tomatoes
¼ cup minced onion
¼ cup chopped pimiento
1 tsp salt
  black pepper
2 Tbsp wine vinegar
2 to 3 cups clear vegetable stock or chicken bouillon
½ cup fresh chopped mixed herbs, such as chives, parsley, basil, or tarragon

Crush garlic in bowl and add bread broken into bits, along with cucumber, green pepper, water, and olive oil. (Don't balk at the bread. It gives the soup a great consistency, and after you blend it, you won't know it's there.) Allow this mixture to marinate for several hours. Then add cut-up tomatoes, onion, pimiento, and salt and pepper. Blend in blender or food processor. Chill thoroughly.

Before serving, mix in vinegar, cold stock, and herbs. Serves 6 to 8.

For added texture, flavor, or color, you may garnish with additional chopped green pepper, cucumber, celery, watercress, garlic croutons, bean sprouts, or lime slices.

QUICK CHICKEN CACCIATORE

½ cup chopped onion
2 cloves garlic, minced
4 Tbsp butter
4 Tbsp olive oil
1 frying chicken, cut up
1 quart tomatoes (fresh or stewed) or tomato sauce
 salt and pepper to taste
½ tsp basil
½ tsp oregano
½ cup dry white or red wine

In a large, heavy pot, sauté the onion and garlic in butter and oil, and add the chicken to brown. Add remaining ingredients and simmer, covered, for thirty minutes or until juices run clear from chicken. Serve with buttered broad noodles and a green salad. Serves 4 to 6.

SENSATIONAL TOMATO QUICHE

½ cup chopped onion
½ cup chopped green pepper
1 clove garlic, minced
2 Tbsp olive oil
2 lbs firm, red, ripe tomatoes
½ tsp each basil, oregano, salt
⅛ tsp pepper
3 Tbsp chopped parsley
1 egg plus 3 egg yolks
3 Tbsp tomato paste
1 partially baked, 8-inch pie crust
12 pitted black olives
⅓ cup grated Parmesan cheese
8 anchovies (optional)

Preheat oven to 350°. Sauté onion, green pepper, and garlic in 2 Tbsp oil in heavy skillet. Add chopped, seeded, peeled tomatoes, herbs, pepper, and parsley. Cover and cook over low heat for five minutes.

Remove cover and raise heat so liquid evaporates. Do not let it scorch. Remove from heat.

Put eggs and tomato paste in bowl and mix well. Combine with tomato mixture and pour into pie crust. Top with olives, grated cheese, and anchovies. Bake until firm and golden, about thirty minutes.

Serves 4 for lunch. Wonderful just with a green salad. Or cut it into a lot of small pieces for excellent hot or cold hors d'oeuvres.

About the
National Gardening Association

The National Gardening Association is a nonprofit member-supported organization dedicated to helping people be successful gardeners at home, in community groups, and in institutions. We believe gardening adds joy and health to living, while improving the environment and encouraging an appreciation for the proper stewardship of the earth.

Established in 1972, this national organization of 250,000 members is now the premier membership organization for gardeners.

Members receive the monthly *National Gardening* magazine, may write the staff horticulturist for help with any gardening problem, receive discounts on gardening books, and get other member benefits. *National Gardening* magazine provides in-depth, how-to articles, profiles of members and their gardens, and evaluations of garden tools and products. Regional articles help members with special climate challenges. The magazine also provides a forum for NGA members in a "Seed Swap" exchange column, and seed and recipe search columns.

The National Gardening Association is a nationwide resource for information, services, and publications related to gardening. Besides the monthly magazine, NGA produces numerous books and directories for the home gardener. NGA also produces the annual *National Gardening Survey*, from research conducted for NGA by the Gallup Organization. This comprehensive report on trends in home gardening in America is widely used by the lawn and garden industry and is cited by the nation's media.

Well known as the information clearinghouse for community garden programs across the country, NGA offers on-site planning assistance, specialized manuals, a network to other organizations, and the annual National Gardening Grant Program—for gardens in neighborhoods, schools, and institutions, especially garden groups for youth, senior citizens, and people with disabilities.

The National Gardening Association continues to explore new ways to gather and share information, to connect gardeners with other gardeners, and to further its mission—successful gardeners everywhere!

If you would like a free sample issue of the *National Gardening* magazine and information on member benefits and how to join the National Gardening Association, please write or call:

The National Gardening Association
180 Flynn Avenue
Burlington, Vermont 05401
(802) 863-1308

Villard's National Gardening Association Series

75000-4 ☐ **BOOK OF TOMATOES**	$4.95; in Canada, $7.50
74991-X ☐ **BOOK OF LETTUCE & GREENS**	$4.95; in Canada, $7.50
74990-1 ☐ **BOOK OF EGGPLANT, OKRA & PEPPERS**	$4.95; in Canada, $7.50
74988-X ☐ **BOOK OF CUCUMBERS, MELONS & SQUASH**	$4.95; in Canada, $7.50

To order, send check or money order (no cash or CODs) to:

Villard Books, c/o Random House, Inc., 400 Hahn Road, Westminster, MD 21157

Please enclose $1.00 for the first book and 50¢ for each additional book to cover postage and handling. Make checks payable to Villard Books. If you have a major credit card, you can charge by phone by calling:

(800) 638-6460

You may also charge to your credit card by mailing in this coupon.

Please send me the books I have checked above.

NAME (please print)

ADDRESS

CITY/STATE   ZIP

PLEASE CHECK ONE: MASTERCARD ☐   VISA ☐
                                              AMERICAN EXPRESS ☐

CARD NUMBER

EXPIRATION DATE

SIGNATURE

Please add applicable sales tax. Allow 4–6 weeks for delivery.